I0682368

RENUNCIATION

A SPIRITUAL STORY

SIMEON HOE

RENUNCIATION
A SPIRITUAL STORY

Copyright © 2018 by Simeon Hoe

All rights reserved.
No part of this book may be reproduced in any manner without
the express written consent of the author, except in the case of
brief excerpts in reviews and articles.

First U.S. Edition, 2018

Cover design by NightOwlFreelance.com
Cover photograph © William Magee

ISBN-10: 1-949193-00-4
ISBN-13: 978-1-949193-00-8

Printed in the U.S.A.

Thank you, Sandy, Steve, Kyle, and Bob.

"With renunciation life begins."
—Amelia Barr

CONTENTS

RENUNCIATION

A SPIRITUAL STORY

INTRODUCTION

"Ross, why do you want me to write about spiritual events I have experienced?"

"Charles, you can be a teacher because of the stories you tell."

"I am powerless over the written word. I feel like I can barely form the simplest ideas into sentences without help."

"Who helps you write your stories?"

"The Creative Spirit of the Universe gives me the words. Words come through me, not from me".

"What happened to bring you to this point?"

"In the simplest terms, I suppose I surrendered. But in the word of the Spirit, I renunciate all power to control my life, as I once understood it. You and I have lost the power to manage, control, determine what is best for us; we just stopped, let go, and yelled, 'Calf rope. I chose God. You chose God.' For me, renunciate is a description of letting go of my life choices. Renouncing control, management of my thoughts and ideas identifies the process I experienced while completely giving myself to God."

"Charles, how does that affect me? I still make plans; keep a calendar; see clients, take care of my mind and body through prayers meditation and healthy eating. I like to think I can control those few things. I still have the power to choose what to wear, eat, my friends, my work."

Ross, you are correct. I think we live an illusion of

manageability. We were given free choice, right? When, in our recovery, we were forced to make a choice. When we decided that God is everything, we renounced our freedom to make choices. I have seen your transformation from disheveled, scattered, spiritually bankrupted person into a man of God, action and purpose. A man who knows himself, likes himself, cares for others, does for others without expectation of recompense".

"Charles, thank you. But what has any of this to do with renunciation?"

"Charles what happened when you chose God over nothing?

"You surrendered your free choice to make major life decisions for yourself just as I have experienced. What's best for the people you love? God makes those choices for me. That's my purpose in life, to do his Will. We do his work; he does our work."

"What does what you say really, truly mean?"

"Charles, that is not possible for everyone. You, I, can't live that way some of the time; we're human. We're wounded. He's perfect. Perfection is not the domain of wounded men."

"Ross, consider that when we meet in a room with other people who are wounded and share our experiences, both painful and pleasant, solutions, or a pathway to the solutions to similar problems is opened. We heal through each other's wounds.

You've witnessed dying men and women fight with God, really angry with God. I watched my mother, wounded by her mother, deny or attempt to deny death because she was angry as hell at God. But when I walked into her room in the hospice wing of the nursing home three days before she died, it was late at night. I watched her. She would seem to fall asleep then suddenly awake,

scanning the wall opposite her bed. Then her eyes would focus on a specific spot on the wall and she would smile, a beaming smile. She focused upon the spot where she saw people who had gone ahead of her, family, friends, lovers, my father waiting for her to join them. I became aware that she and God had gone into a deeply private space where she renounced all her anger, resentments and shortcomings. She again became God's child.

What had mother renounced when she and God became father and daughter? Her resentment of his apparent uncaring when the men she loved were taken away from her or walked out of her life. I was one of those men who walked out of her life. But we each had a part in the process of separation.

"What do you do today that's different from your old life patterns?"

"I find God within me, and stay true to myself, my inner self. Shakespeare wrote, "To thine own self be true," and this is what I plan to do in my spiritual life and let my actions reflect just that."

ONE

There was a spiritual war raging within Charles. He was unaware of the turmoil. He hurt deeply because of something he thought had happened when he was three years old. His parents came to his great aunt's house in San Mateo California. His grandmother told him they had come to spend the night and get up very early the next morning to pick up some horses immediately south of San Mateo and drive back to the ranch.

The next morning Charles, forgetting what he had been told and excited to see his mother and father for the first time, expected them to have breakfast with him. They were nowhere to be found and Charles vowed never to let anyone hurt him as they had hurt him, again.

His expectations had been skewered when he was three.

His mother had given him to his father's mother and her sister to raise him when he was two months old because he was colicky and had projectile vomiting. Molly was unprepared to deal with his problem. Why would this deter a loving mother? Why did his mother give up her only child?

His mother was wounded by her mother who blamed Molly for the pain of childbirth. Molly's wounds prevented the milk of human kindness to flow within her veins. To be fair to Molly's mother, her own mother had died during her birth.

But she did love Charles, very much. She had an odd way of showing her love for him. Charles was fourteen and ensconced in a boarding school in Western Massachusetts when she fell in love with him. Charles' Godmother considered this to be a problem.

The problem was Molly's timing, wanting to cling to him. Molly and his dad had separated, and his father wanted sole custody of his son. The problem was compounded by the fact that Charles pushed back. He did not want to be embraced by a woman who never nurtured or raised him.

Abandoned at two months old into the loving arms of two women who loved

him unconditionally only widened the chasm between mother and son.

However, his mother did not, could not, break the dam that held back the flood waters of motherly love. Nor could Charles accept his mother as she was, a wounded soul.

Eventually, mother and son found one another. He found the mother he had always sought, and she found the strong, bright, loving son she hoped would one day walk into her out stretched arms as she reached for his strength and comfort. That day came. They rejoiced together in the reunion.

Two months later, Molly died, peacefully, serenely with a gentle exaltation of her last breath. A breath so soft and sweet Charles thinks of it as her final song.

The day she died, Molly's room was filled with friends coming to wish her a final farewell.

But only one other person in Molly's room, Charles' wife, had noticed the two women who appeared at the foot of her bed. The sisters Brunilda had materialized.

Two large, Wagnerian women strode authoritatively into Molly's room and stood at the foot of her bed. They wore starched-white uniforms. They looked into one another's eyes, nodded their heads, and with one swift gentle motion lifted the covers back from Molly's ankles. They placed their hands on her ankles, acknowledged one another, removed their hands, put the sheet back over her feet and filed silently out of the room. No one in the nursing home had ever seen them before. They left as mysteriously as they had appeared. Who were these two women?

The two women had been sent by the Holy Spirit. The Spirit had come to take their child home. Home is where we all go. We came from Heaven and we return to Heaven. Molly died.

TWO

What does the story of Molly's death have to do with the civil war raging within Charles' soul? Without the unmet expectations of one July morning in 1946, their conflict and later discovery of one another never would have happened as it did.

Charles' mother and father had left the Grass Valley Ranch in Austin, Nevada and arrived at the home of Charles' great aunt, Mrs. Hussey. Charles's grandmother, Mrs. Hobart (how he referred to her), told him of their coming to the house and the fact that they would spend the night and leave very early the next morning to pick up some horses and drive back to the ranch.

His father backed the International truck with a green cab and a creampuff colored rack, designed to hold either horses or cattle for transport mounted behind the cab up the driveway and into the backyard. Charles was very excited to see the two people he had heard so much about—whose photographs he had memorized—get out of the truck. It was the first time Charles had ever seen his mother and father.

The tailgate had been lowered from the back of the rack to let Charles walk into the back of the truck and see the puppy, Pedro. Charles scrambled up the ramp into the bed of the truck. He stepped onto the straw bedding and was met by the sweetest scent he ever smelled, straw and horse manure. Plus, there was a puppy named Pedro his mother and father were taking to the sheriff of Lander County who lived in Austin, Nevada.

For a three-year-old boy, things could not get any better. The smell of straw and horse manure and the feel and smell of a wiggling puppy was way too much fun.

That evening at dinner, Charles, freshly bathed and well dressed, sat in his usual chair with a cover on the seat cushion to protect the underlying upholstery from spilled food.

There was sterling silver flatware and candle sticks, crystal water glasses, lace place cloths under the knife, forks—two forks, spoon and water glass, finger bowls half filled with water for getting stickiness off one's fingers after finishing a meal, and the dinner plate. There was also a sterling silver butter plate and knife.

Mrs. Hussey sat at the head of the table. Not far from her left foot, if one were to look under the table, was a subtle lump that was a switch that set off a buzzer in the kitchen to summon the cook to bring the various courses for dinner. Charles remembered sitting quietly listening to the adults carry on their conversation.

The next morning, Charles had forgotten what his grandmother told him and expected to see his parents when he went downstairs for breakfast. No parents. Charles walked out of the front door and glared at the spot where the truck had been parked the night before. It was then he promised himself no one would ever hurt him as badly, ever again. This emotional jolt lingered under the surface level of his consciousness and affected every aspect of his life.

THREE

In July, 1948, the Second World War was had been over for three years. Charles had a nurse who was a German refugee. Freda Ingolstadt was her name. She believed young boys should take hardy, disciplined walks, just as the Hitler Youth had trained. And walk they did. They would walk to a park where Freda would meet her German friends or walk into Burlingame. To visit some of the Germans living in the San Mateo-Burlingame area who were survivors of the concentration camps. Once in a while, Freda would meet with other women and one or two would have tattoos of numbers under their left wrist.

At times, Charles felt that Freda had been in the German Army. Their walks were structured and had a purpose. They didn't take pleasant walks at sundown to feel the fog roll in and the temperature fall. When they went anywhere they walked with the purpose of getting to the destination.

Then it happened. One night, Freda put Charles to bed and left the room. Charles did not have his stuffed dog, Corky, in bed with him so he got up and fetched his dog. Freda, hearing him get out of bed, walked into the room and scolded Charles, then took Corky away.

After the third episode, Freda began to beat Charles with her fists. Strong for a three-year-old. Charles escaped and locked himself in his bathroom. Freda beat on the door demanding Charles come out. Charles stayed put until he heard Mrs. Hobart come upstairs. Charles ran out of the bathroom and told Mrs. Hobart what Freda had done to him.

FOUR

One should know Mrs. Hobart's story to appreciate her temperament. Both Mrs. Hobart and Mrs. Hussey, her sister, were two of the first white births recorded in Eureka County, Nevada. Their father, Joe Dean, was a prosperous, tough rancher who traveled to Nevada from New York by sailing around the Horn of South America to San Francisco, California. What took him to Nevada other than opportunity, Charles did not know. Charles later learned that Joe Dean rode to the Texas Panhandle to buy Hereford bulls for his ranches.

In Nevada, Joe Dean operated the Dean Ranch and the Horse Ranch both in Eureka County in North Central Nevada. The two ranches were separated by Mt. Tenabo, the tallest mountain in the range to the west of the Horse Ranch.

On the Western slope of Mt. Tenabo was a very successful

9

silver mine owned and operated by Simeon Wenban, Joe Dean's father-in-law, who had come to the United States from England and temporally settled in Cincinnati, Ohio where he met and married Susan Grace. They had two daughters, Eva and her sister Flora.

The sisters were babies when Joe Dean was killed in a fight over a water hole. Eva Dean, their mother, took them with her to the following murder trial in Eureka, Nevada every day. The sheep man whose last name was Marvel was eventually acquitted.

Charles has Eva Wenban Spencer's Episcopal Prayer Book, but what immediately happened to Eva after Joe Dean was killed remains a mystery. Charles knew one thing, Eva remarried and moved to Oakland, California.

After marrying Susan Grace, Simeon Wenban went to California to answer the call of riches in the California Gold Rush. Living in San Francisco, Wenban joined a partnership in a gold mine he had a hand in discovering. His two partners were dishonest and swindled Wenban out of his share of the mine. From San Francisco, Wenban moved to Virginia City, Nevada and found success in silver mines around Virginia City.

But Wenban was not satisfied with the success he had and traveled west through Central Nevada, the Great Basin, through Austin, Nevada itself: a booming silver town, and west across Grass Valley to Mt. Tenabo where he found high-grade silver ore.

He had three or four other men with him on the expedition through Central Nevada, but the conditions in the Great Basin, and some not too friendly Native Americans, convinced them to turn around. In their absence, Wenban staked claims around the base of Mt. Tenabo and took some ore to Elko, Nevada to be assayed. The ore was, as he thought, high-grade silver ore.

Wenban returned to San Francisco to raise money to operate the mine, buying heavy mining equipment and an assortment of provisions ranging from nuts, washers, bolts, wrenches, vats for acid to clean the matrix off the ore, and essentials to build a house for his wife, as well as camp supplies for the men working in the mine. Investors trusted Wenban. One of his investors was Randolph Hearst who owned the San Francisco Chronicle.

In 1881, Wenban wrote his wife and told her it was time for her and their two young daughters, Eva and Flora to come to the mine located approximately fifty miles Northeast of Austin, Nevada. They traveled by stage coach, river boat, railroad, and covered wagon before arriving in Austin.

They encountered outlaws, stampedes, awful weather and the often times hostile Native Americans, some were Tosowees who eventually became friends with Wenban. Wenban met his family in Austin and took them to the mine. Eva Wenban and her sister Flora had a fine adventure traveling from Cincinnati, Ohio to Austin, Nevada. Native Americans killed some travelers, there were gun fights over almost nothing, rough stage coach travel, highway robbers, as well as the general hardship of travel. When they reached the Cortez Mine, the house their father had built welcomed Susan, Eva, and Flora Wenban.

Simeon and Susan's two daughters spent Summers either at the mine or at their late father's ranch, the Dean Ranch, and attended school in San Francisco in the winter. They both graduated from Vassar College in upstate New York.

After Flora divorced Charles' grandfather, she, along with her young son, moved to the Dean Ranch. Charles' father Randolph Flagg spent summers on the Dean Ranch and the school year in San Francisco, graduating from Princeton in 1928.

Prior to the Depression, Flora ran the Dean Ranch and rode with a gunslinger, Harry Ivester. In the Fall, the cattle would be driven to Beowawe, Nevada where the steers would be loaded into cattle cars and the train would take them to San Francisco. Flora was a very strong and strong-willed woman.

So, when Charles told her that Freda had beaten him she wheeled around and marched downstairs. The next morning Freda was gone. Decades later, Charles forgave Freda.

FIVE

Charles prayed the Lord's Prayer at night with Mrs. Hobart, and often times intuited the outcome of something about to happen in his life. He believed that God was real, but in his subconscious mind Charles never trusted God. He felt it was up to him to do well and to get out of whatever trouble happened upon him, even alcohol-related.

Karl Jung wrote that when a man or a woman reaches middle age, they begin to yearn for the realness of a power greater than themselves to be in their lives. But Charles had always known that there had to be a better way to live life than the way he was living it. Something had to happen to alter the course of his life.

The first item to be renounced by Charles was alcohol.

On the seventh of December in 1983 Charles emerged

from the bedroom in the home of his childhood friend's parents' home freshly dressed. Before walking out of the room, Charles verbalized to himself that he did not want a drink. Walking out the bedroom door and heading straight for the kitchen, Charles stopped at the bar and poured himself a drink.

Backing away from the bar, watching himself in the mirrored glass behind the bar, Charles watched himself take a drink out of the glass filled with what he said he did not want. He was stunned. A light came on and Charles admitted to himself as he studied his reflection in the mirror that he was absolutely powerless over alcohol. Of my own power I cannot stop drinking. The Memorial Service was on the ninth of October in 1983. On Monday the twelfth, Charles met three friends at place where they served "good" hamburgers.

Instead of scotch, Charles drank gin—what his friends were drinking—and a really terrible decision. He got drunk. Before they left the place, Charles and one of the "dancers" were dancing on top of a small round table together.

On Wednesday the fourteenth of December, after one drink, Charles came up with a pitiful excuse he told his wife to avoid going to a friend's home for Christmas Eve dinner. His wife looked at him and went upstairs to call her friend. Charles went into the kitchen to make a second drink.

Think seconds and inches. Walking upstairs to the bedroom, Charles never took so much as a sip from the fresh drink. He walked in the room. His wife turned to look at him.

Her eyes said everything, everything. What were you thinking? How could you have done what you did!? He turned to his right and was suddenly held in place by a flash of light and this message slammed into his brain, "If you ever touch, ever, another drop of alcohol, you will lose everything, everything."

Charles turned and walked into the bathroom and poured out the fresh drink.

Then he walked to the phone and called his psychiatrist. "Ken, alcohol is causing me a problem in my life. What should I do?" Ken told him to go to Alcoholics Anonymous. That night, he walked into an AA meeting as it was winding up. He went back the next night and has never stopped going.

Thinking back, Charles cannot remember where those words, "alcohol is causing me a problem in my life," originated. That was not wording he'd thought before he heard himself say it aloud.

The road to sobriety, grown-up emotional sobriety, was not smooth. Charles fought not to become like one of "them." After fifteen years of fighting, Charles had a spiritual "bottoming out" that saved his life. The road from that point forward was as rough as he made it. And he did a good job of making it rough. Fortunately, for him, Charles was able to let go of and relinquish old ideas, attitudes, and actions. The road began to slowly smooth out.

However, the first fifteen years were not all gunfights and

rebellions. Early on, Charles was befriended by a man from Arkansas who told him more than once to lance the boil that hurt, so "God's light could heal the sore."

There were times when he did lance his own boils, but when he finally helped another man "lance a nasty boil" Charles began to connect spiritually.

His life began to slowly change. The lancing of someone else's boil was a turning point and took place on Maundy Thursday of Easter Week in 1984.

The prior Sunday, Charles went to Sunday School. He liked the woman who taught the small class. What she read from Romans, VIII resonated with him. Hearing that nothing on earth or anywhere else would or could separate him from God's love was very uplifting and settled whatever was making him uncomfortable that morning.

The following Thursday Charles walked into the Psychiatric wing of the County Hospital where he volunteered in the Emergency Rooms. He signed in and said hello to Dr. William Purrier who was the Doctor in charge. They exchanged pleasantries and Dr. Purrier told Charles there was a man in a consultation room he wanted Charles to spend some time with. Charles walked to the end of the short hallway and knocked softly on the door then walked in. He sat across from a man who looked older than he might have been and who was not making much sense. He was weeping and remorseful.

Charles tried to engage the man in some sort of conservation, but the man just sat and sniveled. Finally, Charles used the "lance the boil" approach, and the man began to respond, a little. Charles gently persisted, and the man cleared his throat and looked at Charles for the first time.

"It's a large thing, the big boil."

"Are you ready to let God's light heal the boil?"

"Guess so."

"Tell me, what did you do, or have you done?"

"I molested my daughter."

This was a Black Swan. Charles sat stunned and hoped the daughter looked like the cartoonist's Al Capp's sexy woman, Moonbeam Mc Swine. Why? Maybe, Charles recounted, he could get his head around what the man had just told him if she were, maybe older, more fully developed, anything to lessen the shock of what the man had told him. Though somewhere deep-down Charlies knew that was inappropriate social conditioning as well and there was nothing that could condone such an abusive act against a child of any age. Charles pressed on.

"How old is your daughter"?

"Eight."

Stunned is putting it mildly, then Charles heard the following words come out of his mouth: "You know you're forgiven, don't you?" Where did those words come from? Charles didn't speak those words. They just flowed out of his mouth. Then he remembered the Sunday School class and Roman's Eight about nothing on earth separating us from God's love.

The man asked, "Who forgave me?"

"What season of the year is it?"

"It's Easter."

"Yes, it's Easter, and Christ has forgiven you for molesting your daughter, but the consequences of what you have done sit squarely on your head and shoulders." What Charles later digested about consequences came from reading, 2 Samuel 11:26-12:13. God sent the Prophet Joel to deliver the message of God's chastisement of King David for killing Uriah in order to marry Uriah's wife. The chastisement was direct, accurate and true, but the consequences David had to endure were harsh.

Charles left the man and walked back to the desk where he found Dr. Purrier.

"Do you know what that man just told me!?" The doctor calmly acknowledged what Charles told him and approved of Charles telling the man the consequences of what he did rested solely on the man's shoulders. Obviously, there were more far reaching consequences for the man and his family, but Charles's attention had been focused on the man.

Charles left the Psych ER and retreated to a place where he could digest what had happened to him. Then he called the Episcopal church he and his wife attended and asked to speak to the Rector. The Rector listened to Charles's story.

"Charles, why don't you come to the Maundy Thursday service this evening. I would like to wash your feet."

What did Charles learn in that small consulting room? He

learned about forgiveness. He had always forgiven people, but his forgiveness was superficial, only to distract anger from himself. Forgiveness was not Charles's to give. Charles realized he had only been the conduit for God's forgiveness. Charles had done and said what he would have liked to have forgiven the man for, but that was not possible.

SIX

How does God communicate? Through other people mostly, and sometimes through our dreams. And sometimes God puts us where he wants us to be to learn and to bring love.

Nurses and staff from the other two sides of the Emergency Department, Medicine and Trauma, knew Charles by sight and why he was there. One Thursday afternoon Charles was leaving when a nurse asked him if he would speak with a young woman. The nurse said it was not alcohol related but felt he might help her. The young woman was a senior in high school.

She pulled a prank at the Christian School she attended, and it backfired. She was to graduate at the head of her class and had been accepted at Stanford University. However, because of the prank she had pulled, the school's Head Master punished her by telling her she could not graduate with her class.

She became terrified over the embarrassment to herself and to her family and friends when they heard the bad news that she could not graduate with her class. She slid into the darkness of depression and eventually drank something she hoped would kill her.

When Charles saw the girl, he was struck by how lovely and by how horribly ashamed of herself she was.

Charles sat quietly for a short time before she acknowledged him by raising her head and looking at him. Charles could see she was ashamed for the embarrassment her attempted prank caused her family and friends, and more so because she lived instead of ending her life. When she looked at Charles he introduced himself as Charles Flagg. She gave her name and looked sadly into his eyes. Their eyes began a silent conversation and very soon she began telling Charles what had happened.

What really happened was her maverick spirit got her into trouble. She took it out for a spin and got carried away with some sort of prank that backfired badly.

She began to relax as she told her story, and her shoulders dropped away from her ears. Charles reassured her by telling her that the dust would settle, calm minds would prevail, and she would weather the storm with grace and dignity. The situation would work itself out. Charles smiled. She smiled back. She had a lovely smile.

What was Charles's goal when he spoke with her? Why had he been asked to speak with her in the first place? The question he faced was, how do I replace her negative thinking with a positive outlook on her immediate future and her life moving ahead? What Charles did may best be described as replacing the negative thoughts she had with positive words designed to enable her to have restored confidence and a positive outlook on her life. "Insertive dissonance" was the term Charles coined for how he redirected her focus to the positive. He did this by listening, by accepting her explanation of what happened. He never questioned her motives; he never brought up the subject of the prank. He began to inject positive words to replace the negative, ashamed, embarrassed, and most importantly, move her away from the thought of suicide.

Charles used compassion, empathy, acceptance of who she is on the inside by directing the conversation towards the spiritual solution to her situation. His acceptance of her explanation eliminated any negativity and reinforced the positive.

They spoke for about ten minutes. Before Charles left, they shared a quiet laugh, a nice little laugh.

As Charles got up to leave, the lovely young woman was smiling.

Why had he been asked to speak with her? Charles had been volunteering in the Emergency Department for several years, and people knew him and why he was there. More importantly the staff saw Charles as a very kind, thoughtful, caring man who was solution-oriented.

Word of his positive work in the Psych ER spread. He had spoken to patients in the Medicine side who were being stabilized before going into the Psychiatric side. Those patients had to be physically OK, and Charles liked speaking with these patients when they were unsteady physically. He knew they could be more teachable.

Yes, there were psychiatric patients who were locked in rooms with only one doorknob on the outside of the door, who had been medicated, some more than others. Upon occasion, after some of these patients woke up and were deemed not to be a threat, Charles was asked to go into the room to speak with them. Charles had a message of recovery to share.

Charles was a Lay Eucharist Minister taking the reserve elements, wafers, and a bit of wine remaining from a Communion Services in the Episcopal Church he and his wife attended. At the time, Charles was the head of the Lay Eucharistic Ministers who take the reserve elements to men and women in hospitals, nursing homes, people unable to leave their homes, the elderly.

Charles had returned from making a visit to a nursing home with the husband of a Priest at the church. He took the kit they used for the Eucharistic into the Alter Guild Sacristy and left it for an Alter Guild member to clean. The last service of the morning in the Main Sanctuary was winding down and Charles was walking to the driveway entrance of the church to leave. Suddenly, he heard the receptionist call him back. There was somebody in Room 410 at a local hospital. A friend of the person in the hospital had called the receptionist and insisted someone take him the Eucharist.

Charles returned to the Alter Guild Sacristy and put together another kit. He arrived at the main entrance of the hospital, parked his car, went in and took the elevator to the fourth floor. Turning left as he exited the elevator he stood at the nurse's station introducing himself and explaining why he was there. Looking down the hallway he saw a woman he knew approaching him.

"Charles, I know why you are here, and I hope you can share what you brought." Charles said yes there was plenty of what he had and followed his friend to the room where her husband was. He shook hands with her husband, laid out the elements on a lace cloth spread on the bedside table and began the small Eucharist service.

He began by reading his favorite beginning prayer, "For Today." The man was crying, his wife began to cry, and Charles choked up as he read the prayer. The Eucharist service lasted five or seven minutes. He put everything back into the kit and said a prayer before he left.

As Charles walked out of the room, he looked back to see the number of the room he had visited. The number 410 flew at him as in a three-dimension movie. Charles was surprised to say the least. Going into the room he never paid a bit of attention to the room number. His friend simply led him into the room as they quietly chatted.

Leaving the hospital, Charles was turning left to get onto the main street leading away from the hospital. His cell phone rang. It was the receptionist from the church. She said she had told him the wrong room 410. Charles was supposed to have gone to another wing of the hospital to a different room 410. Charles was stunned. He knew without a shadow of a doubt that God had led him to the husband of his friend who was in room 410 in the main hospital.

His body tingled sharply from his toes to the top of his head. Charles knew beyond any doubt there was a reason why he had gone to the wrong room. God had wanted him to be with his friend and her husband. His friend's husband passed away the next week.

What really happened that Sunday morning? An honest mistake in communicating a hospital wing was made. But who had the greatest need to receive the Body and Blood of our Risen Lord? A man who was dying or a man who had his hip replaced? A friend of the man who had his hip replaced, rattled the receptionist when he called, so she did not tell Charles what building held room 410 the friend was in.

What was the purpose Charles had gone into the man's room? Because the man's wife had guided him there, knowing what was in the kit.

He had set out to comfort a man with the gift of Christ's

Body and Blood. He had no inkling he would be led to the room where the need was the most pressing. Charles did as he was asked. He went to room 410 to comfort a man and a woman in need.

How did he discern who had the greater need?

He did not have to discern anything. God decided.

God wanted Charles in a specific place with a specific person at the County Hospital, just like with the man who had molested his daughter. That event took place during Easter Week of 1984. There was a third event maybe fifteen years later.

Charles was headed home on a Thursday afternoon. He had spoken with two people the doctor in charge of the Psych ER had asked him to see.

He was approaching the entrance to the West ER Medicine, when a nurse approached him and asked him to see a woman the nurse thought to be an alcoholic, based upon the woman's behavior. Charles also learned the woman worked in the administrative offices of the hospital.

He was taken into a treatment room off to the side of the main floor. Charles and the woman were introduced, and Charles began talking about his experience with alcohol. After a couple of minutes, the woman interrupted Charles.

"Excuse me, but you have never asked me what my drug of choice is."

"I was wrong not to have asked. What is your drug of choice?"

"Self-mutilation."

The woman showed Charles the scars on the wrist of her right arm.

Charles was once again stunned. Her response was the very last thing he expected to hear. The nurse who behind them stood in stunned silence. Gathering himself, Charles defaulted to God as the solution for what confronted him.

"Do you believe in God?"

"Yes, I believe in God."

"Do you pray to your God?"

"God only answers honest prayers."

Charles said he felt he had been hit in the chest by the palm of a strong hand. "God only answers honest prayers." Charles had been taught to pray, and Charles believed in God but never trusted Him. By that point in his recovery, Charles had come to trust God, so praying honest prayers made sense in the Universe to him.

He realized that his old way of praying had not always been honest. He immediately knew God had put him in the room with the woman to learn a valuable lesson. Pray honest prayers.

Charles said yes to the nurse who asked him to speak to the woman because he cared. He cared that people suffered from alcoholism and his goal in seeing the woman was to give her hope that in sobriety, a real, vibrant life, was available to her. Instead, he was the one to whom God delivered a message, a lesson, communicating through the most unlikely messenger

Charles had ever met. He thanked the woman and the nurse and continued on his way home.

What really happened? Charles was completely stunned and shaken by what the woman had told him. Charles, at that moment of revelation, stood naked before God. Then came the lesson.

"God only answers honest prayers."

SEVEN

Several years later, Charles was in the church speaking with someone about a friend of his who was in the hospital and wanted to receive the Eucharist. Charles asked if anyone had gone to visit his friend, but no one had taken him the Eucharist. It had been sometime since Charles had taken the Eucharist to anyone, so he went into the Alter Guild Vestry, made up a kit, and left for the hospital. He repeated this process over the weeks until his friend could no longer receive the Eucharist.

A new Rector had come to the church, and his longtime assistant had come with him. Several weeks after the Rector arrived, Charles received a call asking him to meet with the Rector's assistant. To Charles's surprise, he was asked to lead the Lay Eucharistic Minister for the rest of the year. Charles thought himself the least qualified person to be given such an important position in the Lay community within the church.

Charles tended to overdo from time to time. He carried a kit in his car and when visiting a new friend with terminal cancer, not a member of his church, consequences ensued in the form of an email from the Priest who monitored where Charles had taken the Eucharist. She was trimming his sails when she referred to him as a "loose cannon."

Charles was at first furious but kept his opinion to himself. If he was doing God's work taking the Eucharist to those in need, regardless of church affiliation, and had been told to stop doing that, he felt there was something terribly wrong within the Episcopal Church. Time passed and the Priest who scolded Charles became his Spiritual Advisor; the very best Spiritual Advisor he ever had or likely will have. She was eventually called to another church in Raleigh, North Carolina.

"Charles, you've had what I would describe as a variety of spiritual events over the years. Aside from the Priest who had been your Spiritual Advisor who, man or woman, has had the most spiritual impact on your life in recovery?"

The Priest and Charles connected over a book, Salvation of San Mountain by Dennis Covington. It's about the attempted murder trial of a Charismatic Preacher who was on trial for trying to kill his wife. Charles was told the book is, was, mandatory reading for incoming Seminary students at SEWANEE in Tennessee.

One of the most important pieces of advice she gave

Charles was not to put anthropomorphic qualities on God; otherwise, Charles would pigeonhole Him into what he isn't. Today, Charles perceives God as God; He simply is, out "there." Charles was over-intellectualizing spirituality.

One friend suggested Charles listen to a recording of Anthony De Mello, a Jesuit from India. Charles was still fighting the good fight, trying to prove he could be like "normal" people, without drinking when this was suggested to me. What caught his attention the first two times he listened to De Mello was learning that he was not the feeling of the moment, like pain or loneliness' or anger. Those feelings don't define him but exist outside of him."

In 2013 Charles drove to Roswell, New Mexico to meet two other men. On the way, he listed to a workshop Bob and Sandy gave a few years earlier.

He was involved in the alchemist's dream, thinking wetlands could remove the heavy phosphates out of frac water used to drill horizontal oil and gas wells.

He met with people who worked for oil and gas exploration companies and gave a talk to the Geologists Club in Roswell.

Driving home, he listened to the CDs again. He was driving to Big Springs when Sandy said something about Step Ten that made him slow down, pull to the side of the road and call him on the phone. Charles told him he had opened the door to the Tenth Step.

What did he do then?

He thanked God for Sandy's words.

On another CD he heard Sandy say we have to learn how to communicate through spiritual language. A week later, Charles was facilitating a meeting inside a Texas Department of Corrections' prison. So, he tried to address the men in a spiritual language. Something happened during the meeting. He spoke on a subject one man brought up but spoke softly; he shared from his heart. Men were paying attention to what was said.

What did Charles say?

He did not know.

He couldn't remember.

He assumed that was because he was not choosing the words coming out of his mouth. He was in a spiritual zone. When time was up, they circled up for the Lord's Prayer."

How many times has this happened, Charles wondered.

But he was sure he had only had that experience at that particular Unit. Facilitating meetings in other prison groups, large and small, he was busy watching what was going on in the room.

He saw notes being passed between offenders and suspected that there were more than notes being passed around. He has seen what he calls "microprinting," which looks like some sort of code. He used to have to sign offender's sign-in sheets, until one day he noticed a sign-in sheet with what looked like code: gang communications. He put it in his pocket and, after the meeting, gave the offender a new sheet. He asked Charles where his other one was, and

Charles told him it was in his pocket. The prisoner looked unhappy.

Charles had to sign in and out in the Warden's office. When he got there, the warden was in and he handed him the paper, telling him what he thought it could be. The warden turned on his heel muttering, "I've got this handled," and picked up the phone.

From that day forward there are no offender sign in sheets. Hurrah.

EIGHT

The following happened between May and December of 2010. "All day all night, Maryanne…" This was a Harry Bellefonte song from the dark ages and was the first name of a divine lady, Maryanne, Charles first met taking the Eucharist to her in an acute-care nursing home. Maryanne had a nasty infection as well as cancer. There was a message on the door that visitors had to put on a plastic gown, gloves, and a mask. Charles went into the room and saw a black-haired woman who didn't look too well. She smiled and extended a hand as he introduced himself.

They talked a bit as Charles prepared the Eucharist. She was delightful and asked if he would be back the following week. Yes, he would be back. Time passed, and he followed her from another acute care nursing home. Seems people thought

34

she had MRSA, but she did not, and then to her own home where she had a companion, woman, and her greyhound.

Their friendship grew over the months; it perhaps helped that a room in a known hospital was barren except for the bed, bedside table, and one chair. It was big enough to have been a suite in bygone days.

"Charles, what do you think about this room and the hospital?" she asked one day.

"Barren and shabby," was his response.

She agreed.

(To be fair, the hospital underwent a major remodeling and a new modern wing was added, as well as a new Emergency Department.)

While Maryanne was living at home, either before or after the Eucharist, she would talk about growing up outside Amarillo, Texas. She knew how to drive a team of horses and was involved in most every aspect of ranching and farming. She had a wonderful mind. Beginning either in late October or early November, her health began to decline. Charles could see her decline before his eyes with each subsequent visit. Sometimes they would talk about her health and other times talk around it, focusing on whatever in her life brought her joy and happiness.

In early December, her caretaker would help her walk from her bedroom to the living room where she would visit with Charles and share the Eucharist. Then came the day when her very nice caretaker told Charles Maryanne did not want to see anybody. A week before Christmas she died.

Christmas Eve 2010.

In 2010, Charles was a Chalice Bearer at his Episcopal Church, and he had signed up to serve at the Christmas Eve children's afternoon service. He loved to watch the process to the alter when the priest invited them as he read the Liturgy of the Eucharist. He had done the same thing the year before and it was a joyful service.

The men and women in the Alter Party processed in and took their seats. He was seated perpendicular to and on the right side of the alter as seen from the congregation. The service proceeded and before the priest began the liturgy, he invited the children to join him at the Alter. He was surrounded by children, but as the kids came to the Alter Charles saw a person who had recently died, last one moving forward, process up the steps through the children and into the Alter. She did not reappear. "She" was Maryanne.

His eyes were riveted upon her face as she moved forward, like a child with Maryanne's face. To say he was stunned would be an understatement, but he intuitively knew why she appeared to him. Maryanne wanted him to know she was in God's hands, safe, whole, living in Eternal Life.

CONCLUSION

"Charles, how have you digested what you saw and became aware of?"

"Ross, I had completely forgotten the event. Who could I tell without someone thinking I was certifiably nuts? I shared the story with the priest who was at the Alter, but his response was neutral. I told my wife and she understood, but after telling her I did not share the story with anyone else."

"Why not?"

"That's not a story for people who do not accept spiritual events as spiritual events. Some people are not willing to see things in other than black and white when the world is really technicolor, including the paranormal. Ross, Evil is real, and evil really exists, so do the mysteries that make God's world so magnificent. They exist side by side, but by choosing to see things in the light of God's love, evil remains at bay."

"Why do you think the priest's response was neutral? How do you really feel about it in hindsight?"

"Dr. William Silkworth wrote that he thought men of science were not fully aware of the powers of good that lay beyond our synthetic knowledge. When I finally became aware of what he meant by the powers of good that reside beyond my synthetic knowledge, the Universe opened its doors to me. I wanted to experience some of those powers of good, personally."

"Were you able to do that?"

"Yes."

"How?"

"Ross, I prayed for an open mind to receive those powers of good without realizing that before I could receive anything I had to renounce those defects of character that prevented me from receiving. I learned through mistakes, ass-chewings, and listening to people. I listened to AA speakers either on old cassettes, CDs or by attending speaker meetings and regular meetings. Prayer and meditation were very helpful, but what was most helpful arrived when I realized that serving at the Alter for ten plus years was ego driven, not motivated by my heart and soul. I had a distorted sense of reality, and until that problem was resolved, God knew I was too immature to experience anything until I knew the truth that existed buried within me. Not the truth about myself delivered by other men.

"But what about those events you shared when you were volunteering in the Psych ER?"

"Looking back, I realize they were learning experiences. How to pray, how to forgive, how to do a number of things without expecting anything in return. Gradually, I gained experience, and experience became wisdom, regardless of how painful the experience was. 'Pain is the touchstone to growth.' Growing up in public was very painful and a lesson in humility."

"Charles, aside from learning the hard way, what would you consider one of the more important lessons you have learned while on your spiritual path?"

"Ross, first I had to discover the kernel of anger that resided below the level of my consciousness. If you count the first moment this was lodged in my psyche, it's been almost seven decades.

Mrs. Hobart told a three-year-old me why my parents were coming to San Mateo. They were coming to see me and to pick up two horses early the next morning and drive back to the ranch outside Austin, Nevada. When I finally remembered what I had been told when I was three, I spoke with my sponsor who seemed to think I was on the right path.

Then I went to speak with a psychiatrist. As we spoke about what happened, I felt myself going down a rabbit hole, ending up next to the three-year-old me, glaring at the driveway where the truck stood the night before.

I asked the child if he had been able to give voice to how he felt that morning. "No," was the reply. I asked him if I could speak for him. He said yes. I spoke for him and out poured the angry words a three-year-old could not have said. Then, as quickly as I had appeared next to the child, I was sitting in an armchair in the doctor's office. The kernel had been removed: rage."

"Go on—you mentioned three things that happened to bring peace to your life. You are a healer, Charles, and you have to stay calm if you are going to help people. You told me you have a resentment against formal religion, what's that about?"

"I have come to a place of peace about that resentment.

When I least expected it, an understanding was given to me. Remember I spoke about the powers of good that exist beyond our synthetic knowledge?"

"I do. How does that fit?"

"Ross, I believed that if I am open to those powers of good, they would lead me into a deep, rich, spiritual life. The example I have is Christ who taught in riddles, parables, but lead by example. I can follow his example by the actions I take to serve others. Christ said in one of the Gospels that we have the power to move mountains if our faith is strong enough.

I believe the mountains those powers of good move are the boulders of resentment that reside within me. Instead of focusing on the negative things that happened in the name of religion, I simply accepted what had happened. I didn't have to like what happened but accepting all the horrible things that did happen in the name of religion changed its meaning. The resentment was gone."

"You are telling me the powers of good that exist beyond our synthetic knowledge can do all that?"

"Yes."

"Thank you, Charles."